PET OWNER'S GUIDE TO THE
Jack Russell Terrier

SECOND EDITION

John Valentine

RINGPRESS

Published by Ringpress Books,
a division of Interpet Publishing,
Vincent Lane, Dorking,
Surrey, RH4 3YX, UK.
Tel: 01306 873822   Fax: 01306 876712
email: sales@interpet.co.uk

SECOND EDITION First published 2003
©2003 Ringpress Books Limited. All rights reserved

ISBN 13   978 1 86054 293 0

Printed and bound in Hong Kong through Printworks International Ltd.

CONTENTS

1 INTRODUCING THE JACK RUSSELL

Most people will have come across a small, white, docked terrier, which is referred to as a 'Jack Russell Terrier'.

As far back as the end of the 18th century, there is pictorial evidence of a white-bodied, or predominantly white-bodied, terrier of the type known today as the Jack Russell Terrier. Few of today's popular breeds of dog can be reliably traced back as far as this in an unchanged state.

A Terrier Named Pitch

There is an engraving by Scott that portrays a terrier, called Pitch, which was published in 1810. It is taken from an oil painting by Sawrey Gilpin.

This depicts, unmistakably, the type of terrier that was to be favoured by the Reverend John Russell, the man who gave the breed its name in the 19th century.

Pitch was born around 1785 and was owned by Colonel Thornton. The dog is shown to be white-bodied with the characteristic head and tail markings. He may appear a little deep in the chest for the breed enthusiasts of today, but he is still quite typical of the breed of terrier that is now recognised as the Parson Russell Terrier.

The Reverend John Russell

John Russell, the founder of the Jack Russell breed, was born in 1705 in Dartmouth. His father was Rector of Iddesleigh in North Devon. He was a keen huntsman, an interest that his son was swift to develop. Inevitably, this led to an involvement with the type of terrier used for bolting foxes.

In 1819, John Russell, who was by then a curate, acquired a terrier from a milkman. The terrier was known as Trump, and this dog has gone down in history as the first Jack Russell Terrier. This was the start of John Russell's lifelong interest in developing the sporting

companion, and Trump left a legacy of game, sporting little terriers, bearing the Parson's name, that are highly prized to this day.

The breed still carries the stamp of the Rev. Russell's terriers.

A PORTRAIT OF TRUMP

An oil painting of Trump, by Mary Palmer, was painted in the Parson's own lifetime, and he reputedly regarded it as a good likeness. It shows Trump as being white-bodied, with head and tail markings similar to Colonel Thornton's Pitch from the previous century. She was described by John Russell's curate, E.W.L. Davies (who wrote a book called *The Outdoor Life and Times of John Russell*), as having a patch of dark tan over each eye and ear, with a similar dot, not larger than a penny piece, at the root of her tail. Her coat was thick, close and wiry, to protect from the wet and cold, and her legs were as straight as arrows, with her whole frame indicative of hardihood and endurance. Her size and height are compared to that of a full-grown vixen fox.

THE TERRIER'S WORK

The name 'terrier' is generally accepted as being derived from the Latin 'terra', meaning earth. The Jack Russell Terrier was bred to go to ground, i.e. to work in the earth, for the purpose of bolting foxes.

The terrier's work is to go to ground.

John Russell required that his terriers were not only of conformation to enable them to go to ground after the fox, but also that they possessed the stamina and build to be able to keep up with the hounds.

Dogs also needed the stamina to keep pace with hounds and horses.

The Rev. John Russell: founder of the famous breed of terriers.

THE END OF AN ERA

When John Russell died on April 28th 1883, in his 88th year, he had devoted more than 60 years of his life to breeding foxing terriers like Trump. During this time his reputation as a breeder of terriers, and as a huntsman, had become widespread.

The Reverend John Russell was buried at Swymbridge, in Devon, where his funeral was attended by at least a thousand people. The Parson was not only a respected breeder of terriers – he was also well liked and respected by his parishioners.

THE JACK RUSSELL'S HERITAGE

Carlisle Tack, born in 1884, and therefore only one year after Parson Russell's death, is portrayed in a drawing by Arthur Wardle.

Tack's pedigree shows that he was descended from some of John Russell's own terriers, and, although lacking in the head and tail markings of Trump, he shows a definite similarity to that first terrier acquired some 65 years before.

Fashions in the show ring may alter the appearance of a breed in the space of a few years, but nature's changes are seldom as dramatic. The type of terrier required today to bolt a fox from its earth is the same as it was during the Reverend John Russell's own lifetime and before.

Terriers looking just like Carlisle

Tack can still be seen at both conformation shows and hunt shows alike. However, the decline in blood sports means that fewer terriers are seen today in the field.

The decline of blood sports means there are few working terriers left.

Official Recognition

In 1990, the Parson Russell Terrier achieved official recognition from the British Kennel Club, and has subsequently received recognition from equivalent bodies abroad.

For many years prior to recognition, the Jack Russell had its faithful band of enthusiasts, with breed clubs organising their own shows. But there was no official Breed Standard, and so the breed deviated in type.

A shorter-legged dog also became popular. This type is still very much in existence today, but is not officially recognised by the British Kennel Club.

In Australia, the Australian National Kennel Council (ANKC) recognises both the

The short-legged Jack Russell is a popular companion dog.

Parson Russell Terrier as it is recognised in Britain, and a shorter-legged variation, with Australia being regarded as the country of development for the smaller variety. Meanwhile, the number of Parson Russell Terriers registered continues to grow.

As official recognition for the breed continues to spread, the number of Parson Russell Terriers seen competing within the mainstream of canine exhibitors increases. The Russell is truly an all-round breed; it is successful in breed competition, at Agility and as a working terrier, and it has also gained worldwide popularity as a family pet.

11

THE BREED STANDARD

The Breed Standard issued by the Kennel Club for the Parson Russell describes the 'ideal' dog in terms of coat, conformation and temperament.

POINTS OF THE JACK RUSSELL

Stop

Occiput

Withers

Back

Croup

Tail

Muzzle

Chest

Tuck up

Stifle

Hock

Pastern

General Appearance

Built for size and endurance, the Parson Russell Terrier should appear active and agile. The length of the body should appear slightly more than the height of the dog.

Characteristics

Essentially a working dog, the Russell must be of the correct build to enable him to "go to ground" after foxes. He must also have the stamina to "run with hounds".

Head

The skull should be flat and moderately broad. The muzzle should be slightly shorter than the length from the stop (the point between the eyes) to the occiput (the point at the back of the skull).

Eyes

The eyes should not be set too far apart. They should be dark, almond-shaped and deep-set.

Ears

Ears should be small, V-shaped, carried close to the head and of moderate thickness.

Nose

Black in colour, with good-sized nostrils.

Mouth

Strong jaws, thick lips, and the teeth should meet in a scissor bite (the upper teeth closely overlapping the lower).

The keen, alert expression of a typical Russell.

Forequarters

The shoulders should be well angulated, long and sloping, giving maximum reach in front. Elbows should be straight and perpendicular to the sides, and legs should be straight.

Body

The chest must not be too deep, as this would prevent a dog following his quarry underground. It should not extend below the elbows at its deepest point.

The topline should arch slightly over the loins, and flow into the tail.

Hindquarters

Strong and muscular. The hocks should be short, and straight when viewed from behind, giving maximum drive.

Agile and athletic, but small enough to go to ground.

The contrast between the rough- and the smooth-coated Russell.

Feet

Compact feet, with tough pads to protect them over rough ground.

Tail

By custom the tail is docked, but with the increasing restrictions on docking, more Russells sport a full tail. It should be of good thickness from root to tip.

Movement

Movement should appear effortless, with the terrier covering maximum ground with minimum effort.

Colour and Markings

The colour can be all-white or white with markings of lemon, tan or black, or a combination of these, i.e. tri-colour, with the markings preferably being confined to the head and root of the tail.

Coat

The coat can be rough, broken or smooth, but there should always be a dense, soft undercoat and a harsh, straight topcoat.

Size

The Russell should be of similar dimensions to a full-grown vixen fox. The ideal height is 14 inches (35cms) for a dog, and 13 inches (32.5cms) for a bitch.

THE JACK RUSSELL CHARACTER

In temperament, the Russell should be bold and friendly, with no aggressive or nervous tendencies. He should be biddable and even-tempered while in the presence of other dogs and livestock.

He is an active, alert, intelligent little dog. Full of life, the ever-inquisitive Jack Russell will investigate any hedgerow or ditch whenever the opportunity presents itself. This is a dog that needs plenty of exercise and mental stimulation if he is to be kept happy.

Equally at home whether in the town or the country, providing the Russell is properly housed and exercised, he will provide his owner with many years of devoted loyalty and untroubled enjoyment.

The adaptable Russell is equally at home in the town or the country.

OWNING A JACK RUSSELL

A hardy terrier, the Russell is free from many of the hereditary afflictions associated with so many of today's pedigree breeds of dog.

However, before embarking on the search for a puppy, you should be sure that this really is the breed for you.

It is a terrier, and, like all terriers, the Russell has a strong but rewarding personality. This is especially the case since the Russell is still bred as a worker, and retains many of the attributes first bred for in a terrier.

The Russell Terrier is a breed with brain, and there is no doubt that he will know how to use that brain to his best advantage. But, handled and trained correctly, the Russell will make an excellent family pet.

A breed with a strong but rewarding character.

2 CHOOSING A JACK RUSSELL

Having given your choice of breed much consideration, and decided that the Parson Russell Terrier is the breed that you definitely want, you will need to obtain a list of breeders.

Your national kennel club will be able to supply you with a list of breed clubs and their secretaries, who in turn should be able to supply you with details of breeders, or club members, in your area.

As with many other breeds, all breeders will have certain characteristics unique to their own breeding plans. It is, therefore, important to see as many examples of the breed as possible, in order that you can make a well-informed decision.

Assessing the Litter

When you visit the breeder, there are many factors to evaluate before getting down to choosing a puppy. The puppies should be kept in a clean environment, and all members of the litter should be clean, bright-eyed and lively.

Make sure that you see the mother of the puppies with her

The puppies should be kept in a clean environment.

litter, along with any other adults that the breeder may have. If possible, you should also try to see the father of the puppies.

Some bitches will lose a little condition after whelping, but will never look neglected if they have been properly cared for. Always try to buy a puppy from a reputable breeder who has extended care and attention not only to the rearing of the puppies, but also to any adults he or she may have.

Unlike tins on a supermarket shelf, puppies are not always conveniently available

Make sure you see the pups with their mother.

when you want one. A great many reputable breeders will have a waiting list for puppies, and you may be added to the list.

This will allow both the buyer and the seller to have thinking time to make a well-informed decision, either way, before the puppy is purchased.

Remember, this is a decision that you are going to have to live with for the rest of the dog's life – and that will probably be the best part of 15 years, or perhaps more. Taking your time now can save a lot of heartache later on.

You may have to wait until a pup is available.

THE PERCENTAGE GAME

In the search for a reputable breeder, and in turn for a puppy, it is also important not to be too influenced by the achievements in the show ring of any particular 'kennel'. The number of wins, if you are interested in them, should always be compared to the number of puppies produced by that breeder, giving a percentage of winning Jack Russell Terriers from the number of puppies bred. In a truly successful 'kennel' the number of puppies produced doesn't need to be too high for the breeder to make a mark on the show scene.

TEMPERAMENT

If you are not intending to show your puppy, the prime consideration must be temperament. A dog's character is not, as is sometimes thought, exclusively the result of the owner's rearing and training programme.

Temperament is an inherited characteristic, and, while the puppy's experiences may mould the temperament for better or worse, they will only alter the underlying character of the dog in a very minor way. Russell puppies should always be forthcoming and friendly, and a healthy puppy will always be bright-eyed and full of life. Try to pick the type of puppy that will fit in with your lifestyle. If you, for example, have a busy lifestyle with a lot going on, it is best to go for the puppy that is out-going, taking everything in his stride. For the quiet person, a very boisterous puppy is not going to make the best companion.

Do take time to consider your choice of puppy. Many of the adult Jack Russell Terriers that end up with breed rescue societies do so because they did not suit their owners to begin with.

Take time to pick out the pup that will suit your lifestyle.

CHOOSING THE RIGHT SEX

The sex of the puppy is really of little relevance if you are looking for a pet. It is largely a matter of personal preference.

If you choose a bitch, you will have to cope with her seasonal cycle, making sure she is kept from male dogs when she is on heat. The male dog may show signs of slightly antisocial behaviour during adolescence, such as 'mounting' legs or cushions, and some adult males have a tendency to wander.

Unless you plan to breed, it is advisable to neuter your dog, so that any of the problems commonly associated with either sex will be eliminated.

If you plan to show or breed, it may be better to start off with a bitch. You then have the option of improving on your bitch by taking her to a good stud dog. In this way, the puppies should improve on any of their mother's faults.

You must make your intentions clear so that the breeder can help you to make the correct choice.

The choice of male or female Russell comes down to personal preference.

COAT AND COLOUR

Russells may have smooth, broken or rough coats. The colours are tan and white, black and white, and tri-colour, although white should always predominate. Most pet owners attach little importance to coat and colour, as the main priority is to find a healthy puppy, with a sound temperament.

THE RIGHT PUPPY FOR YOU

If you have found a reputable breeder, it is well worth listening to his or her advice when it comes to choosing a puppy.

The breeder has had the opportunity to observe the puppies closely over a number of weeks, and will have found out about their individual characters, as well as evaluating their conformation.

A good breeder will know the puppies and should be able to point new owners towards the most suitable puppy for their lifestyle. It is important to be clear in your mind as to what you are looking for. Is your puppy solely to be a pet? Are you likely to be interested in showing or breeding from your puppy when he or she is older? If you are looking for a show-quality pup, make this clear to the breeder.

Even in the most carefully planned and well-bred litter, there will be some element of variation in quality among the puppies and in their outlook on life. Only the very best specimens should be bred from, and the potential show dog will need careful choosing.

Sometimes, through no fault of his own, an older dog or young adult may need re-homing. Before embarking on the search for a puppy, it is a good idea to consider whether an older puppy or an adult Russell may be more suitable for your circumstances.

There are various reasons that could lead to the adult Jack Russell finding himself in need of a new home. It could be the result of a marriage break-up, the owner may have become too

ATTRACTIONS OF

ill to care for the dog, or, sometimes, the dog outlives his owner.

In the majority of these cases, the Jack Russell will be of a perfectly suitable disposition for a pet. The advantages of re-homing an adult dog are that there is no need for house-training, the dog will have grown out of his destructive, chewing puppy stage, and the terrier's character and temperament will be fully developed.

It may also be worth considering taking on the older puppy or adolescent. It is common practice among breeders to 'run on' the best two or three from the litter until they are six months or so, perhaps even 12 months or so.

Such puppies will, more often than not, be of sufficient merit

In some situations an older dog may be a better option.

AN OLDER DOG

to have warranted being 'run on', and although the breeder will be keeping what he believes to be the best puppy, those that are sold subsequently will still be good examples of the breed.

This is particularly relevant if your intention is to show the puppy, as his potential as a show dog may not always be easy to assess before the age of six months.

By the age of five or six months, the puppy will have his adult dentition, and the mouth can be checked to ensure that the bite is correct for the breed and that a full set of teeth is present.

The advantages of acquiring a puppy at around six months of age are that the puppy will already be fully inoculated, he will probably be house-trained, and he may well have received preliminary training as a show dog. Again, he will have outgrown the chewing stage.

It may be that a breeder has a retired brood bitch that he or she wishes to re-home. In a large kennel, it is the kinder option to allow this type of dog to enjoy the comforts of a family home.

Even at nine years old, a Russell will still have a good few years of life left, and this may prove an ideal solution for the elderly owner.

You can make an accurate assessment of an older dog's show prospects.

GETTING READY FOR YOUR RUSSELL

Preparations must be made in advance for the arrival of the new puppy or the adult Russell. If you are getting a puppy, both your house and your garden should be made safe.

Inside the house, check for trailing electrical flexes, and make sure, as far as possible, that any precious objects are kept out of reach. Make sure the garden is securely fenced, and also check that there are no gaps in the hedges where an inquisitive puppy could crawl through.

Before you go to collect the puppy, ask the breeder for a diet sheet, so that you will be able to stock up with the type of food to which the puppy has become accustomed. If you have decided to take on an adult Russell, you should also find out what diet the dog is used to.

Dog Bowls

You will need two bowls for your dog – one for drinking water and one for food. The best type to buy is the stainless-steel variety. They are easy to clean and last a lifetime.

Make sure the bed a puppy's you buy can withstand chewing!

Beds

There are various styles of dog bed on the market, and most will be suitable for the Russell. However, it is important to remember that puppies are inclined to chew during their teething stage, and any bed bought for the puppy may need to be replaced when the puppy is older.

For this reason, it may be advisable to use a cardboard box (ensuring it is free of metal staples) for the first couple of months. This will be perfectly comfortable as long as it is lined with washable bedding material.

The bed should be placed in a warm, draught-free corner where the puppy or adult will be able to enjoy some element of privacy.

GREAT CRATES

Crates are becoming increasingly popular, and many dog owners find them invaluable. Although they are expensive, they are virtually indestructible and will provide a 'home' for your dog throughout his life. The advantage of a crate is that the puppy can be confined at night and for short periods during the day. The puppy soon learns to accept his crate as a safe haven, and will go into it at will. If you stay away from home, the crate can be packed up and taken with you, ensuring that your dog will settle happily in a strange place.

COLLARS AND LEADS

As soon as your puppy has had a chance to settle, he will need to start getting used to wearing a collar. To begin with, this should be soft, perhaps made of rolled leather.

Obviously, you will need a bigger collar as your puppy grows, but this can be purchased at a later stage. You will also need to have some form of identity disc to attach to the collar.

Your puppy will not be allowed to venture beyond the garden until he has completed his vaccination course, but you can practise lead-training in the garden (see page 54).

There is a wide variety of leads to choose from, made from many different materials. It is advisable to start with a light, nylon lead, which the puppy will scarcely notice.

When he is bigger, you will probably want to graduate to a leather lead.

This is much kinder on the hands, particularly if your puppy has a tendency to pull. Chain leads may look smart, but they are not user-friendly for the handler.

Whatever lead you choose, make sure it has a secure trigger fastening, as the Russell, although small, still has considerable strength.

Your pup will be confined to the garden until he has completed his vaccinations.

MAKE A PLAY   FOR TOYS!

Toys need to be provided for both the new puppy and the adult Russell.
There are a great many dog toys available from pet shops and dog
shows. While the vast majority of toys will provide your pet with some
degree of enjoyment, the specially designed orthodontic toys will
aid the puppy's teething and help with the dental care of
the adult Russell. Any toys that your Russell is
going to be left with should be
strong and safe.

VACCINATIONS

It is a good idea to consult your veterinary surgery in advance to enquire about the procedure for vaccinating puppies.

Puppies need to be vaccinated against parvovirus, leptospirosis and canine hepatitis. A rabies vaccination is required in some countries.

The first vaccination is usually given at between eight and ten weeks, and will be followed by a second at least two weeks later. Some practices will also give the puppy a third injection at about the 18-week stage.

Before your puppy has been fully inoculated, he should not be taken beyond your house and garden.

COLLECTING YOUR PUPPY

At last, the big day arrives when you are ready to collect your puppy. If you are travelling by car, it is a good idea to take a friend or a member of the family with you to hold the puppy on the return journey.

Take a towel for the puppy to lie on, and some paper towels in case of accidents.

Timing

Arrange with the breeder to collect your puppy reasonably early in the day, as this will give your puppy time to adapt to his new home before night-time.

When you collect your puppy, the breeder should provide you with a diet sheet (if this has not been sent to you already). Many breeders will supply a small quantity of food so that the puppy does not have to experience a change in diet, no matter how minor, for the first few meals.

If you are purchasing a pedigree Parson Russell Terrier, you will need the relevant paperwork from your national kennel club.

On the journey home, make sure the puppy is held firmly, or is confined in a crate.

Hopefully, the breeder will not have fed him prior to the journey, so he should not suffer any ill-effects. Some puppies may salivate or drool when they first travel in a car, and so the paper towels may well come in very handy.

At last it is time for your puppy to come home.

ARRIVING HOME

The new puppy has so much to get used to when he first arrives home. Everything is strange, and he has left the security of his mother and litter-mates.

Allow your puppy to explore, first in the garden, and then take him into the kitchen, or wherever he is to sleep.

Introduce members of the family in a calm manner, and avoid the temptation of inviting all your friends and neighbours to meet the new arrival.

If you already have a dog or a cat living in the house, introductions must be supervised closely. Make sure that the older dog does not have his nose put out of joint by making too much fuss of the puppy. Equally, it is important to make sure the puppy

Introductions should be calm and relaxed.

does not tease the older dog. In most cases, the older dog will give a warning growl, and the puppy will learn to respect him.

Do not be worried if your new puppy refuses to eat the first meal you give him. He will be distracted by his new surroundings and will probably not feel settled enough to eat. Make sure he has fresh water to drink – and he will probably make up for his temporary loss of appetite at the next mealtime.

THE FIRST NIGHT

This can be a testing time for both puppy and owner. The best course of action is to settle your puppy in his bed or crate, and close the door on him.

Nearly all puppies will make a fuss at being left. They miss the warmth and companionship of their littermates, and they have yet to settle into their new home.

Make the bed as comfortable as possible, with an old toy to snuggle up to (making sure the eyes or any other potentially dangerous parts have been removed). You could also provide a covered hot-water bottle to keep the puppy warm. However, your puppy will almost certainly voice his protests, and it is just a matter of leaving him to it. In fact, he will be so tired after his traumatic day, he will settle down to sleep, eventually.

It is very tempting to get up and comfort your bewildered little puppy, but you could be making a rod for your own back.

If your puppy learns that a loud protest on his part results in attention from you, he will continue to cry every night. If you are deaf to his cries, he will soon learn to settle down to sleep.

A puppy will settle far more quickly if he has a crate.

If you are consistent with house-training, your pup will soon get the right idea.

HOUSE-TRAINING

This is another aspect of taking on a puppy which most owners dread, but, in fact, house-training is a perfectly straightforward procedure if you stick to certain guidelines.

- Select an area of the garden that is to be used for toileting purposes. Make sure you always take your pup out to this spot.
- Use a command such as "Be clean", and when he performs, give lavish praise. In time, your pup will learn to associate the command with what is required.
- Have a little game with your pup before you take him inside again. If you rush back in, he may employ delaying tactics to stay out longer.

- Your pup will need taking out at the following times:
  - First thing in the morning
  - After a meal
  - After a play session
  - After a nap
  - If you see your pup sniffing or circling
  - Last thing at night.
- It is important to be 100 per cent consistent in taking your pup out at these times. If he makes a mistake, it is your fault for not being vigilant.

If you have taken on an older dog that has been used to living in a kennel, he may need time to adjust to living in the house. However, he will quickly grasp what is required.

3 CARING FOR YOUR JACK RUSSELL

Nutritional requirement should be one of the main considerations for the Russell owner, particularly during the vital growing period.

It is absolutely essential that a puppy receives an adequate diet, to ensure the correct and healthy development of the teeth, bones, skin, muscles and coat.

In order that any deficiencies be avoided, it is probably best to feed your puppy on a good-quality proprietary brand of pet food, designed especially for the puppy or junior stages of growth.

When feeding a 'complete' diet,

make sure that fresh drinking water is available at all times. If the decision is taken to feed your pup on fresh meat, then the use of a supplement for puppies and growing dogs will be necessary.

Most puppies start with four small meals a day from eight weeks of age, often divided between meat and cereal feeds. By 12 weeks, this can be reduced to three meals and, by the time he is five to six months old, to two meals a day. When he is a year old, your Russell can have the feeding routine reduced to one meal a day, fed either in the morning or evening.

Until the age of six months, your puppy will need to be treated for the roundworm *Toxocara canis* with a suitable compound, taking care to follow the manufacturer's instructions for administration.

When your puppy receives his initial vaccinations at 8-12 weeks, you can ask your vet to recommend a worming programme.

Puppies are often wormed again at six months with an all-purpose worm treatment, which also eliminates the tapeworm *Dipylidium caninum*. Thereafter, follow your vet's advice regarding worming.

Discuss a worming programme with your vet.

TEETHING

The 'puppy teeth' will begin to fall out from as early as 12 weeks, starting with the middle incisors. The deciduous teeth will be replaced by the adult teeth over a period of two to three months.

This seldom causes any problems, but the puppy should be checked to make sure all the deciduous teeth have actually come out. Sometimes, the adult canine teeth will fail to push the puppy canine teeth out, resulting in 'double' teeth. However, if the puppy is encouraged to chew on hard biscuits and chew-sticks, this should help the milk teeth to come out.

SOCIALISATION

This is possibly the most vital part of a puppy's all-round education. In the first 12 months, you should ensure that your Russell encounters as many different experiences as possible.

This will generally involve a great many short walks in busy streets while the puppy is still young, in order to accustom him to traffic and to people.

If you do not have children in the family, make sure your pup has the opportunity to play with some who are used to dogs.

He should also meet other dogs and get used to livestock. Take care when introducing your puppy to other dogs, ensuring that all meetings are friendly ones. A bad experience at an early age could reflect on his outlook later in life.

A puppy that is carefully socialised will give the owner few problems when he is an adult.

Exercise

Exercise for the young puppy should be limited, as he needs time to develop physically before being given the rigorous exercise enjoyed by many adult Russell Terriers. It will be obvious when the youngster is showing signs of tiring, and this is the time to curtail exercise.

The adult Russell Terrier thrives on exercise. He is a lively, inquisitive, agile little dog, and he will enjoy investigating new walks whenever possible.

Your pup should be exposed to as many different situations as possible.

GOING TO GROUND

When exercising your Russell, make sure you know the areas well. This is a dog that is still led by his instinct, and there is always a danger that he may attempt to 'go to ground' and then become trapped.

A CARE ROUTINE

A lot of work is involved in caring for a Russell's coat – guidance is given in Chapter Four. But there are a number of routine checks you should make to ensure your dog is fit, clean and healthy.

Teeth

On a weekly basis, your Russell should have his teeth and gums examined for signs of tartar build-up, damage to his dentition, and gum disease.

If necessary, the Russell's teeth should be cleaned with a toothpaste and toothbrush designed for canine use. The toothpaste will usually be of a meaty flavour, and most dogs do not object to it.

Gums also need to be checked for any signs of gum disease.

Regular brushing will keep the teeth clean.

Ears

The ears also need to be checked regularly, and, if necessary, cleaned using a proprietary cleansing fluid and cotton-wool. Be careful not to probe inside the ear, as you could do serious damage. Limit cleaning to the area that is visible.

The use of an aural cleansing solution will help to bring any dirt and wax from deeper within the ear to the surface, so that it can be cleaned effectively.

EAR MITES

If the ears have become infested with ear mites, treat with insecticidal ear drops. Ear mites will cause the dog a lot of distress. He will frequently shake his head and scratch at his ears, often whimpering at the same time. Seek veterinary advice to ensure the problem is not more serious.

THE IMPORTANCE OF EYE CARE

The eyes must be kept free from dirt. Each day, the inner corner of the eye should be carefully wiped with a damp ball of cotton-wool. The main causes of eye infection are usually dirt that has got into the eye, or a draught where the dog has been sleeping. Occasionally, a terrier may have a foreign object in his eye, which may or may not cause distress. Likewise, it may or may not be visible to the owner. If a weeping eye has not cleared up within a couple of days, veterinary advice should be sought without delay.

LOOKING AFTER NAILS AND FEET

Nails should be checked regularly to see if they need to be trimmed. If your Russell is exercised regularly on hard surfaces, and the feet are of the correct shape, the nails should not need to be trimmed.

However, incorrect feet or inadequate exercise on hard ground may mean that the dog's nails will need to be cut from time to time. If you are not confident about cutting the nails yourself, ask your vet, or someone who has plenty of experience, to help.

Feet

The skin around the top of the nails needs to be checked for signs of infection. If the skin around the pad looks particularly red or swollen, seek veterinary advice. Often, problems with feet occur when the terrier does a lot of running on hard ground or frequently digs in the earth.

During the summer months, check the feet regularly for signs of grass seeds between the toes. If these go unnoticed, they can cause an abscess. Similarly, the underside of the pads also need to be checked for grass seeds.

Pads can become cracked or split, usually resulting in lameness. This needs to be checked to ensure that the lameness is not being caused by a foreign object that has penetrated the pad. If in any doubt, contact your veterinary surgeon, who will be able to give you the best advice.

Enlist expert help when you first trim your Russell's nails.

THE ELDERLY JACK RUSSELL

Most Russells will keep in good health as they grow older. The average life expectancy of a Russell is about 15 years, with many reaching 18 and sometimes 20 years old while still in good health.

The weight of the veteran Jack Russell will need to be more carefully monitored, as a veteran will be more inclined to put on weight, and it is harder to get the excess pounds back off again.

The best practice is to change the dog's diet to a suitable alternative for the ageing dog. Many pet food ranges offer a 'senior' variety. However, most Russells remain quite active as they age, and this must also be reflected in the dog's diet.

If your Russell is gaining weight easily and you are having problems keeping his weight down, this is an indication that it may be time to change the diet.

Special Care

The teeth of the veteran Russell will need to be checked more regularly for signs of decay and damage, particularly to the carnassial teeth at the back of the mouth.

Exercise for the veteran Russell should not necessarily be restricted just because of age, providing the terrier is still keen

We are fortunate that the Russell is a long-lived breed.

to go for walks. If he appears tired by the amount of exercise he is being given, it should be reduced accordingly.

Pay extra attention during routine checks for anything that seems untoward. In most cases, early diagnosis will ensure that any problem is rectified successfully.

Let your elderly Russell decide how much exercise he needs.

THE FINAL PARTING

Unfortunately, dogs do not live as long as humans, and losing a beloved companion is an inevitable part of dog ownership. In the majority of cases, dogs do not die naturally. We can intervene to put an end to suffering and this is often the best course of action to take. It is, without a doubt, the hardest decision a dog owner has to face, but it should be viewed as part of the responsibility of caring for a dog. If your Russell has got to the point when he is in pain, and he has lost his quality of life, it is time to put him to sleep. Ideally, you should ask the vet to come to your house, so your dog does not have the trauma of going to the surgery. Your old friend can be eased out of this life while being stroked and comforted in familiar surroundings. Of course, you will miss your old dog, but, in time, you will be able to look back on all the happy times you spent together.

4

COAT CARE

Grooming is an essential part of caring for your Jack Russell. The main purpose is to keep his coat clean and in good condition, but it also gives the opportunity to examine your dog on a regular basis.

In this way, you will be able to spot any signs of trouble at the earliest stage – and so any treatment required is likely to be more successful.

The amount of grooming that your Russell will require depends on his coat type. There are three varieties:

- Smooth-coated
- Broken-coated
- Rough-coated.

Rough-coated (left) and broken-coated (right).

In all three types, the coat should consist of an undercoat and a topcoat. The topcoat will vary in length depending on the coat variety, but the undercoat should always be the same – short, soft and very dense.

The topcoat should be hard and straight, ideally lying flat to the body, giving good protection from the elements.

Smooth-coated.

TRACING THE REAL RUSSELL ROOTS

The Reverend Thomas Pearce, writing in the 1870s, describes the coat of his terrier, which was bred by the Reverend John Russell.

"It is rather long, very hard or harsh, and yet perfectly smooth; his legs are clean, and the whole profile of the dog is sharp and defined.

"The peculiar texture does not interfere with the profile of the body, though there is a shaggy eyebrow and a pronounced moustache. The eyebrow is a great mark, giving the dog the look of a Bristol merchant."

Obviously, the smooth-coated Russell will lack the characteristic eyebrows and moustache, but this makes the smooth-coated Russell no less correct in breed type. The eyebrows and moustache should grow naturally and should not need to be the result of skilful trimming.

GROOMING REQUIREMENTS

A good Russell coat should only need brushing to keep it clean. The natural oils present in the coat should act as a repellent to dirt and water, keeping the terrier's skin dry should he find himself out in the rain.

Although the Jack Russell should be groomed regularly throughout the year, whether smooth-, broken- or rough-coated, he will require more grooming in the spring months

Grooming should become a part of a regular routine and

presents the owner with an ideal opportunity to check the terrier for signs of parasites, such as fleas.

During the regular grooming sessions, any long hairs that grow upwards from in front of the eyes should be removed. Simply grip the hair between your finger and thumb and pull it out.

In spring, the Russell will begin to shed his winter coat, resulting in an increase in the amount of hair found around the house and in the dog's sleeping quarters.

Smooth Coat

If your Russell has a smooth coat, there will be no coat to strip out and grooming is relatively simple. Using a slicker-brush, the coat should be brushed against the pattern of growth to remove any loose hair and dead undercoat. The dead undercoat will appear in

A regular grooming session gives you the opportunity to check over your dog.

the brush as soft, downy hair. Do not use a slicker-brush that is too hard, as this will scratch the dog's skin and will make grooming an unpleasant experience.

After removing the dead undercoat, the topcoat should be rubbed with a damp cloth or damp hands, first against the pattern of growth, and then with the direction of growth.

This should remove the loose topcoat. However, the process may need to be repeated a number of times before the terrier has finished shedding.

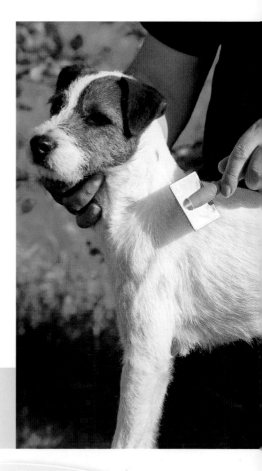

Routine grooming of the rough- and broken-coated Russell will suffice until it is time to strip the coat.

THE BROKEN/ROUGH COAT

In the spring, the broken- or rough-coated Russell will need to be stripped out by hand. Without stripping, the coat will fall out in time anyway, but if it is all stripped out at once, it will grow in more neatly, and there will be less hair left lying around the house. There is no need to bath the dog prior to stripping, though it will do no harm to wash the dog after he has been stripped.

HAND-STRIPPING: A COMPLETE

- The coat should be prepared in the same manner as the smooth-coated Russell, using the slicker-brush. The loose undercoat will be removed with the slicker-brush, but the topcoat will need to be removed by hand.

- Start at the back of the neck, and, using your finger and thumb, grip the hair near the base.

- Pull the hair away from the dog in the direction that it is growing, making sure you do not pull out the undercoat. If the coat is ready to come out, this should require little effort on the part of the owner – and it will not hurt the dog. If the coat does not come away when pulled, it may not yet be ready to be stripped and should be left for another week or so.

- Providing the terrier's coat is coming out easily, continue to pluck out the hair from the back of the neck, always pulling in the direction of the growth.

- Continue over the shoulders, along the back, and towards the tail. The coat will be heavier

TOP: A coat ready for stripping.

LEFT: Use a slicker brush to remove the loose undercoat.

STEP-BY-STEP GUIDE

around the neck and over the shoulders if your Russell has the correct coat.

● When you have removed all the hair from the neck and the back, the hair under the throat and down the tummy will need to be removed. If the growth on the undersides is quite heavy, it may be better to do it a little at a time. If the process is very time-consuming, it can be done over a couple of days.

● For neatness, any long hairs on the underside of the tail should be removed, using finger and thumb. Also check for any straggling hairs that may interfere with the profile of the dog.

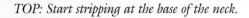

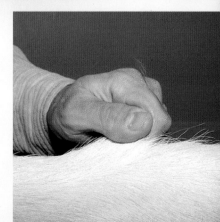

TOP: Start stripping at the base of the neck.

CENTRE: If the hair is coming out easily, progress to the shoulders.

RIGHT: Continue stripping along the line of the back.

ABOVE: Move to the underside, and tidy up the hair around the elbows.

BELOW: The long hairs on the tummy will need to be stripped.

● Use a small pair of sharp scissors to trim the hair around the genitalia. Scissors can also be used to cut any long hairs around the outside edges of the feet. Do not trim over the top of the feet or the nails, as you will leave unsightly scissor marks.

Once the broken- or rough-coated Jack Russell has been stripped out, he will resemble the smooth-coated variety. A new coat will begin to grow through about six weeks or so after the dog has been stripped, but it may be a

Tidy up the tail.

good few months before the dog has regained his full coat.

If your Russell Terrier has an extremely heavy coat, or a particularly soft coat, it may not be suitable for stripping. If in doubt, seek the advice of someone with experience of grooming who can assess your dog's coat for you.

The clean outline of a stripped Russell.

SHARP   PRACTICE

It is important to keep a pair of scissors specifically for trimming your Russell's coat. Ideally, these should be small, round-ended scissors, specifically designed for trimming dogs. They can be bought at trade stands at the bigger dog shows, at large pet stores, or from grooming parlours. It is important to have good scissors, and it is also important to keep them sharp. Blunt scissors leave a poor finish and they are also more likely to contribute to making errors.

BATHTIME

A good, correct Russell coat, whether smooth-, broken- or rough-coated, does not need to be bathed in order to remove everyday dirt. The natural oils in the coat should ensure that any mud and dirt that the terrier picks up when out walking will drop off when dry.

Brushing with a good-quality slicker-brush should be all that is required to restore the coat's whiteness.

Of course, not all dirt and mud is odourless – and occasionally, bathing may be necessary.

There are times when your Russell really needs a bath!

- Use a good-quality, mild dog shampoo and follow the manufacturer's instructions.
- Remember to have dry towels on hand. If possible, shower the dog, as this is swift and effective.
- Leave the head dry to begin with. Soak the dog's body with luke-warm water, and then apply the shampoo, working it into the coat.
- Rinse the body throughout, making sure no trace of shampoo remains.
- Next, wet the head and apply shampoo, taking care to avoid the eyes and nostrils.
- All shampoo must be thoroughly rinsed off before the dog is dried.
- The undercoat will take some time to dry out completely, and, unless the weather is fine, your Russell will need to be kept inside for a couple of hours until he is dry.

50

5 TRAINING YOUR JACK RUSSELL

A s with any breed, praise is an important aspect of successful training. Most dogs will be eager to please their owners to some degree, and it is this aspect of the dog's nature that the owner must take advantage of during training at all levels.

The importance of keeping commands short and simple must also be stressed, as this is the key to success. The dog's understanding of human vocabulary is very limited, and, although some dogs do show remarkable intelligence, your pet is unlikely to understand long-winded commands and sentences.

EARLY LEARNING

While serious, intensive training should not really begin until about six months of age, the way you have reared and socialised your puppy prior to this will have a bearing on how he reacts to noise and other distractions. It is important to introduce your puppy to the noise of traffic and the hurly-burly of the outside world as soon as he is vaccinated. Even if you carry your puppy, he will still be learning. This stage of socialisation is vital for all puppies.

TRAINING EXERCISES

It is essential for both owner and dog to be in a relaxed frame of mind during training sessions if the exercise is to be successful. Try to avoid training when your puppy is likely to be hungry, or amid other distractions that may result in your Russell's mind being elsewhere.

The Sit

This is an easy exercise to teach, and you can start as soon as your pup arrives in his new home.

- Hold a treat above your pup's nose, and as he looks up, he will naturally go into the Sit position.
- Reward your pup, and try the exercise again. This time, as your pup goes into the Sit, give the verbal command. It will not take long before your pup associates the word "Sit" with the action.
- If your pup is a bit slow on the uptake, you can apply gentle pressure to his hindquarters to encourage him to go into the Sit. Remember to give plenty of praise and then release him.
- You can reinforce the Sit command at mealtimes by holding the puppy's bowl above his head. As he looks up, he will

Hold a treat above your pup's head to encourage him to Sit.

go into the Sit position. As he does this, give the command "Sit" and place his meal in front of him.

- Follow the same procedure each day and it will not be long before your Russell responds instantly to the command.

The Down

- To teach your puppy the Down position on command, first put him in the Sit.
- Lower a treat towards the ground. Your pup will follow his nose, and will try to get the treat, which should be held at ground level in a closed fist.
- As your pup tries to get the treat, he will lower himself into the Down position. Wait a few seconds, and then reward him with the treat and lots of praise.
- Next time, give the verbal command, as your pup goes into position.

Lower the treat towards the ground, and your pup should follow it, going into the Down position.

- Repeat the exercise once or twice again after about five minutes or so, and end the training session with plenty of praise.

MAKE SURE IT'S FUN!

It is very important that your puppy does not become bored during training. The exercises should be fun to learn and rewarded with praise.

LEAD-TRAINING

The first task is to introduce your puppy to wearing a collar.

- Wait until your pup has settled into his new home, and then try putting a soft, leather collar on him.
- Make sure you have a toy close at hand so you can distract his attention when he starts to scratch at it.
- In most cases, the puppy will soon forget that he is wearing the collar. Leave it on for a short while and then try again the next day. Gradually extend the time the puppy is wearing the collar until you can leave it on full-time.
- The next step is to attach the lead. To begin with, allow your pup to go where he wants, letting the lead trail. Supervise him closely to ensure the lead does not get caught on anything.
- Now pick the lead up, and hold the end, still allowing your pup to go where he wants.

Use a toy or a treat, and encourage your pup to follow.

- You must now try to encourage your pup to follow you when he is on the lead. A toy or treat can be used as an incentive.
- If your pup seems a little reluctant, recruit a helper and ask them to call the pup's name. When he responds, run with him.
- Remember to give lots of verbal praise and encouragement when your pup responds correctly.
- Never yank or pull your puppy, or he will soon regard the lead as a form of punishment.
- Build up your lead-training with short walks in the garden.

You can practise lead walking in the garden.

By the time your puppy has completed his vaccinations, he will be ready to walk out confidently on the lead.

TEACHING THE STAY

This is an important exercise to teach as it ensures you have control over your dog in all situations. It is easier if you start off with your pup on the lead.

- Start with your pup in the Sit or the Down, and give the command Stay, as you step one pace in front of your pup.
- Back up the command by giving a hand signal, holding your palm flat, facing the pup.
- Wait a few seconds and then return to your pup's side, give a treat, praise, and release him.

55

- Repeat the exercise, stepping a couple of paces away from your pup.
- Build up the Stay in easy stages, until you can walk to the end of the lead, and wait before returning to his side.
- When your pup is steady in the Stay on-lead, progress to doing the exercise with your pup off-lead.

Use a hand signal to reinforce the Stay.

ALL ABOUT THE RECALL

When your pup first arrives in his new home, he will be quick to learn his name, and will be keen to be with you. Capitalise on this, by practising fun recalls. All you have to do is call your pup's name, add "Come", and as soon as your pup reaches you, give him a treat.

Capitalise on your puppy's instinct to follow.

When you start working on a more formal Recall, it may help if you have a friend or a member of the family to assist. At the very least, you will need a good length of rope if your Russell is to be prevented from taking some extra free exercise.

Work at building up a really enthusiastic response to the Recall!

Make sure that the environment you choose for training is free from distractions and from any possible hazards.

- To begin with, put your Russell in a comfortable position such as the Sit.
- Using your hand to back up the command "Stay", step back two or three paces from your puppy, with your helper holding on to the lead, or keeping hold with a length of rope tied to the collar.
- Now give the command "Come", sounding bright and enthusiastic. As soon as you give the command, your helper must release the pup.
- As soon as your pup gets to you, give him a treat and plenty of praise. The distance you can leave your puppy can be increased as he becomes familiar with the command.
- If your Russell makes a bid for freedom as you step back, put him back in the same position and repeat the exercise.
- If he keeps breaking the Stay, it is better to stop, have a game, and then try a simple exercise, such as Sit, where success can be guaranteed. End the training session on a positive note, and try the Recall exercise the following day, when, hopefully, your puppy will be in a more responsive frame of mind.

TEACHING YOUR JACK RUSSELL

The gundog breeds, such as Labrador Retrievers and Golden Retrievers, are bred to retrieve and they will need very little encouragement before they are fetching everything in sight!

This is not the case with the Russell, and you will need to use a combination of treats, verbal praise and patience to get results.

The retrieve exercise is probably the most difficult exercise for the novice owner to teach. The vast majority of Russells will enjoy chasing a moving object, and this must form the basis of teaching the retrieve.

If your puppy is interested in chasing a ball, or any other toy, the only additional element is to teach him to bring the object back to you.

● Introduce the command "Fetch" when you throw the toy and your puppy runs after it.

● When your pup picks up the toy, give the command "Hold", and encourage him to come back to you. Do not distract him too much or he will drop what he is carrying.

● Once your puppy has returned to you with the toy, praise him and then throw the toy for him again. In this way, the exercise becomes a game that the dog will enjoy, which will make him enthusiastic to respond to the retrieve command on all occasions.

TOP: Start by getting your Russell focused on a favourite toy.

CENTRE: When you throw it, introduce the command "Fetch".

BOTTOM: Now call your dog so that he brings the toy back to you.

TO RETRIEVE

NEW CHALLENGES

The Russell is a bright, intelligent dog who likes to keep busy. Mental stimulation is just as important as physical exercise, and so think of ways of channelling your Russell's energies.

Good Citizen Awards

This is a scheme run by the Kennel Club to promote good manners and responsible ownership. There are three tests: bronze, silver and gold, with an increasing level of difficulty.

Many clubs now include the award scheme in their training programme.

Mini Agility

Once you have a good level of control over your Russell, you could consider having a go at Agility. This discipline is an obstacle course where the dogs compete against the clock. Mini Agility is specially designed for smaller breeds, and the fit, athletic Russell will thrive on this challenge.

PROBLEM BEHAVIOUR

As with any breed, problems may arise with an individual Jack Russell Terrier, resulting from temperament and behaviour. Problems may vary depending on the lifestyle, environment and age of the individual concerned.

Behavioural problems may be of a basic nature, as seen in many dogs from a variety of breeds, or they may be more serious and deep-rooted, possibly resulting from the terrier's breeding.

Aggression

Aggression in the individual dog can manifest itself in many ways. When the aggression is directed towards other dogs it may be territorial, which is more likely in the male Russell – and particularly common in the male Jack Russell that has been used for breeding.

Aggressive behaviour towards other dogs can also be the result of fear. If your Jack Russell lacks confidence, he may well attempt to 'bluster it out' with other dogs. Fortunately, this type of

nervousness can often be overcome.

The best course of action is to take your Jack Russell to training classes, where he will meet other dogs and gradually become more confident. This is also relevant if your Russell shows nervousness when approached by people. The more he meets people in controlled situations, the more likely he is to overcome his fears.

Territorial aggression can be solved by neutering (see page 65),

Despite your best efforts, problems can arise.

TUNING IN

It is important that you remain calm and confident, despite any aggressive tendencies displayed by your dog. For, more often than not, it is the owner's behaviour that lies at the root of the problem. If the dog senses fear in his owner, his response will be to defend his owner. Unchecked, the dog will take the 'appropriate' action towards whatever he sees as being the threat. This scenario often becomes a vicious circle in which the owner becomes more tense and apprehensive as another dog approaches, and the terrier becomes more intent on defending his owner.

if the animal is not used for breeding. In the majority of cases, this will alleviate the problem considerably.

This type of aggression can be a problem in a busy household with frequent visitors. If this is the case, it is advisable to keep the dog in a separate room or in his crate until the visitor is in the house. The dog can then be introduced calmly, and he will not feel as threatened as when greeting strangers on the doorstep.

DOUBLE TROUBLE

Aggression between two or more Russells in the same household can become a terrible problem for the owner.

If there are bitches and dogs kept in the same home, aggression may develop between the males when the bitches are in season. This may or may not rectify itself when the bitches go out of season, but sometimes the dogs' dislike for each other may become quite intense.

If the problem is dealt with before it is allowed to get to this stage, severe animosity can be avoided. The dogs should be separated when the bitches are in season, and, if any of the adults – dog or bitch – are not being used for breeding, they should be neutered.

Once an intense dislike has developed between two dogs, they will seldom become reconciled. In this situation, it is advisable to keep the dogs separate at all times, or to re-home one of them.

Bitches may also display aggression towards each other at different stages of their oestrus cycle. However, providing they are of a good temperament, they will settle down once their hormones are back to normal. If any of the bitches concerned are

Maintaining harmony between dogs can be tricky.

not being bred from, it is best to have them neutered.

If two Jack Russell Terriers become engaged in battle, it is important that the owner remains as calm as possible. The terriers should not be pulled apart if they have a good grip on each other, which will often be the case. If possible, immerse the pair in water or throw water in their faces.

Most fights between two dogs will seldom become very serious, and it is often possible to separate the two by shouting at them and asserting your own position as the 'pack leader'.

AGGRESSION TOWARDS PEOPLE

A dog who shows aggression towards people can pose a considerable threat – and, in many cases, this deviant behaviour is directed towards the dog's owner.

Incorrect training will usually be the root of such a problem, as the Russell has a misplaced sense of dominance over the owner, and the owner – who may be afraid of the dog – has failed to rectify the problem.

Once established, this can be a difficult problem to resolve. The best course of action is to enrol in training classes for the benefit

of both dog and owner. It may also be worthwhile to seek the help of a qualified animal behaviourist.

GOING AWOL

The Russell's love of hunting can lead him into mischief. Sometimes, he will run off into the bushes and fail to return when called. Some terriers will remain there for quite some time.

If the dog fails to come after he has been trained, on future occasions he should remain on the lead, and only be allowed to run free in suitable 'distraction-free' environments.

If your Russell wanders away from home, as can be the case with some male Russells in search

You must be able to control your dog when he is off the lead.

of bitches in season, the problem will be rectified by neutering. A straying dog causes problems not only for the owner, but also to the general public and other dog owners.

CHEWING   IT OVER

Chewing is most commonly the result of boredom, except during a puppy's teething stages. If a Russell is likely to be left for some time without human company, it may be an idea to purchase another dog to keep him company in the absence of the owner. However, two dogs can get up to more mischief than one, so they must be provided with their own toys. The Russell that likes to chew, even when he has company, needs further training and his own playthings.

BASIC DISOBEDIENCE

Basic disobedience is usually the result of inappropriate training, perhaps as a result of the owner's ignorance. Training classes will help to train the dog correctly, or, more precisely, to train the owner.

Remember that training classes are there to assist with problem dogs, so, no matter how embarrassing it may be to work with a disobedient dog, it is worth persevering. Providing you listen to the advice given, and train your dog at home as well as at the training class, you will achieve your goal eventually.

Training classes are there to assist with any problems you may

A dog that keeps breaking the rules has lost respect for his owner.

have, and to teach you the correct way in which to train your dog. The trainer will not train your dog for you – that is your job.

THE CASE FOR NEUTERING

Neutering the male Russell may solve a multitude of problems, including leg-lifting around the house, mounting people's legs, and aggression towards other dogs. In the bitch, neutering will solve the temperamental problems that may arise from oestrus-orientated hormonal changes, such as those that arise during a false pregnancy. There are also a number of health benefits that should be considered. The best plan is to discuss the subject with your vet before making a decision.

6

HEALTH CARE

The Jack Russell Terrier is a tough little dog, bred to work in demanding conditions.

As a result, this is a breed without exaggeration, who will suffer few major health problems.

In fact, the Russell is particularly long-lived, and many live beyond 14 years, still enjoying a relatively active life.

Prevention

Preventative health care is vital in caring for your dog, and it is for this reason that a regular routine of checking your dog is highly recommended (Chapter Three).

If you know the signs of a healthy dog, you will be quick to notice any abnormalities, such as small lumps or swellings, or any change in behaviour. The owner can become finely attuned to his

dog, and spotting trouble at an early stage can be of enormous benefit if treatment is required.

A well-balanced diet is also important in keeping your Russell healthy. This should vary depending on your dog's age and the amount of work he is doing or exercise he is taking.

Beware of over-feeding your Russell, as obesity is the prime cause of many health problems. Over-feeding is not a kindness. It can – and frequently does – curtail your dog's life expectancy.

DON'T FORGET YOUR FIRST-AID KIT

All responsible owners should keep a first-aid kit for those occasions when your dog needs immediate treatment. In most cases, this will be for dealing with minor problems, such as cuts and grazes.

In more serious cases, you will need to seek veterinary advice at the first available opportunity. In the first-aid kit you will need:

- A blunt-ended pair of scissors
- Cotton-wool (cotton)
- A mild disinfectant
- Sterile dressings
  (these can be purchased individually wrapped)
- A roll of surgical tape
- Antiseptic wound powder
- Antiseptic wound ointment.

Most veterinary practices will sell antiseptic products, and will be more than happy to advise on a first-aid kit.

COMMON AILMENTS

During the course of the Jack Russell's life, he may succumb to a variety of common ailments. The majority of these can be treated effectively and without much expense if they are spotted early and the appropriate treatment is administered.

In all cases, seek veterinary advice if you are worried about your dog's condition.

Anal Glands

The anal glands may need to be attended to from time to time. These are situated either side of the anal passage.

The anal gland has a duct opening into the anal canal at the anus. The glands secrete a rather foul-smelling substance and may, from time to time, become blocked.

The terrier will be seen to be licking at, or trying to lick at, the anal passage. He may drag his back passage along the ground in a bid to relieve the irritation. Occasionally, if unattended, the anal glands may become infected, in which case the dog will require immediate veterinary attention.

The glands can be emptied by applying pressure at either side of the anus. However, it is advisable to leave this to someone with experience – it should not be attempted by the new owner. If the anal glands cause persistent, recurring problems, surgery may help to relieve the dog's suffering.

If you spot problems at an early stage, they are much easier to treat.

Bites and Wounds

If your Russell sustains a wound, it is vital that he receives first-aid treatment as soon as possible. Antiseptic compounds are only effective if used in the first couple of hours.

If the wound is particularly deep or if it is bleeding profusely, it may need stitching and a course of antibiotics from your vet. If the wound becomes red, swollen or inflamed, even after first-aid, a course of antibiotics may be required.

Coughing

Some dogs seem particularly prone to coughs. In most cases, the quicker your dog receives attention, the quicker the recovery will be – and the dog is less likely to develop complications. Veterinary advice should be sought, as the coughing may be the result of an obstruction.

If the cough is allowed to go untreated, the illness will become more serious, and your dog will most certainly need a course of antibiotics.

Diarrhoea

If your Russell has diarrhoea, and no other accompanying symptoms, he should be given no food for 24 hours, allowing access only to fresh water. When you resume feeding, provide chicken or fish for the first couple of meals.

However, if the condition is no better, or if it worsens at any time, consult your veterinary surgeon.

Ear/Eye Infections

Infections in the ear or the eye may be caused by a foreign body, such as a grass seed. Eye infections can worsen very quickly, so you should seek veterinary advice without delay if you are at all worried.

If the eye is runny, it may be that your dog has been sleeping in a draught. Bathe the eye with cotton-wool and warm water, and move the dog's sleeping quarters. If the condition does not improve, seek veterinary advice.

Insect Stings

Bee and wasp stings can have potentially fatal consequences. Bee stings are commonly left in the recipient, and, if visible, should be carefully removed.

If your dog has been stung in the mouth, it is best to seek veterinary advice without delay.

If the tongue begins to swell, you will need to ensure that it does not restrict the dog's airway. If you are at all concerned about your dog's behaviour, consult your vet.

A foreign body in the eye can lead to infection.

REMEMBER... HEATSTROKE CAN BE LETHAL

Heatstroke is a problem to watch out for in warm weather. Never leave a dog inside a car on a warm day. Unlike a human, the dog has no ability to sweat through the skin. As the external temperature rises, dogs pant to cool down.

In the case of a dog shut inside a car in warm weather, as the external temperature continues to rise, the dog will become increasingly distressed. To begin with, the dog will salivate heavily, and will become unsteady on his feet. If the temperature continues to rise, the dog will collapse and die.

Kennels and runs should always have adequate shading from strong sunlight.

If your Russell is found to be suffering from heatstroke, his body temperature will need to be reduced as quickly as possible. Immersing him in cold water, or covering the dog in cold, wet towels is quick and effective. As soon as you have administered first-aid treatment, consult your veterinary surgeon as soon as possible.

ECTOPARASITES

This term applies to those parasites that live outside the dog's body. If left untreated, any ectoparasite may lead to severe irritation, resulting in acute distress and hair loss. If in doubt about any skin condition, consult your veterinary surgeon.

A keen eye, accompanying a regular grooming programme, should ensure that any suffering caused by parasitic infestation will be kept to a minimum. An insecticidal spray or spot-on treatment will give protection against a number of ectoparasites, including fleas, lice, mites and ticks.

Fleas

Fleas are a common problem in the summer. They can be picked up from a number of hosts – other dogs, cats, hedgehogs and foxes are all possible sources of fleas. Providing the signs for fleas are checked for

regularly, the treatment of these little parasites is relatively straightforward.

The terrier's coat should be checked regularly for signs of flea infestation in summer and in winter. If you can find fleas in your Russell's coat, it is likely that he has a great many. Fleas are visible to the naked eye, although they move through the dog's coat at some speed.

Flea droppings, which normally resemble small bits of grit, can be

Fleas can be controlled by using a spray.

seen, especially near the base of the tail and under the back legs. The flea dirt, when splashed with water, will change to a red colour. The flea droppings are usually accompanied by the onset of intense scratching by the terrier.

If your Russell is seen to be scratching, he should immediately be checked for signs of fleas. The adult flea will lay up to 200 eggs per day around the dog's living quarters. These will grow into the adult flea after going through a larval stage, feeding on organic matter.

The adult flea feeds on the blood of its host and can cause severe irritation. It can also be responsible for the transmission of tapeworm.

If you find signs of fleas, your Jack Russell will need to be sprayed with a suitable insecticidal spray, as should any other dogs in the house, or any cats, taking care to avoid the eyes and possible inhalation by the dog or the handler.

The bedding will also need to be sprayed with a household

Spot-on treatment for fleas will last for a couple of months.

insecticidal spray, as will any carpets and other soft furnishings. The initial treatment for fleas should also be accompanied by treatment for tapeworm.

During warm weather, it is advisable to adopt a policy of regular preventative treatment for fleas, always taking care to follow the instructions for the use of any insecticide carefully.

Harvest Mites

Mites can be a common source of irritation in the summer. They come from a variety of sources.

The bright red larvae of the harvest mite can be seen in between the dog's toes, and around the eyes and the ears. They feed on lymph and skin tissues causing irritation to the dog. A regular check should be made, particularly if the dog is seen chewing and licking at his feet. Once again, treatment with a suitable insecticide will be necessary.

Lice

Lice can be seen in the coat as small greyish flakes resembling dandruff. The eggs (nits) are laid directly on the coat, and will appear to be stuck to the hair.

Lice can also be responsible for transmitting tapeworm in the dog, and so the initial treatment will need to be accompanied by a treatment for tapeworm.

Mange

This is a particularly irritating affliction, caused by mites, and it needs immediate attention. Demodectic and Sarcoptic mange are two forms of common, non-host-specific mites.

Dogs that live in the country may pick up harvest mites.

Treatment can be lengthy and should be carried out under veterinary supervision. This could involve antibiotics and the application of medicated washes. Positive diagnosis is made with skin scrapes, which are viewed through a microscope. Treatment needs to be thorough if the mite is to be eradicated.

Ticks

Ticks may not be as common as fleas, but they are more likely to cause infection.

The adult tick has specially designed mouth parts, which enable it to attach itself to the host, where it then feeds on the host's blood. As the tick gorges itself on the blood, it will become more evident, and will usually cause the skin around it to become red and swollen.

Ticks need to be carefully removed, making sure that the mouth parts are not left embedded in the skin.

The best way of doing this is to apply an antiseptic or some insecticidal spray to the tick. This will cause it to lose its grip on the skin. In some cases, the removal of a tick may need to be accompanied by a course of antibiotics.

It is essential to remove the whole tick, or infection may result.

ENDOPARASITES

This term applies to parasites that live inside the dog's body. Although there are treatments to eradicate worms, the best course of action is to adopt a routine worming programme, which should keep your dog free from major infestation.

Roundworm

Toxocara canis (roundworm) is a problem more relevant to the breeding bitch and the puppy under six months old. *Toxocara canis* larvae can affect humans and may cause damage to human tissues.

Puppies that are infested with roundworms appear pot-bellied, and, if they are carrying a heavy burden of worms, they will also lack condition. Worming with an appropriate compound is essential.

Tapeworm

The tapeworm *Dipylidium caninum* may affect the adult Jack Russell Terrier throughout his life,

Routine worming is essential for your dog.

and will need regular treatment with a good proprietary worming compound. Tapeworm segments can be seen around the dog's anus, resembling small grains of rice. Fleas carry tapeworms, which infect the dog when the flea is ingested, making worming essential if the dog has been known to harbour fleas.

Tapeworms can also affect humans, and a regular routine for worming the adult dog should be adopted by the owner. Make sure that the guidelines for administration of the worming compound are carefully followed.

FAST RELIEF

Vomiting in a dog that generally appears to be otherwise lively and healthy should be treated with a 24-hour fast to give the stomach a rest. Make sure fresh water is available at all times. If, after 24 hours, the dog continues to vomit, or if the condition worsens at any time during this period, seek veterinary attention without delay.

INHERITED CONDITIONS

There are a vast number of hereditary defects associated with small dogs that may, or may not, be relevant to the Jack Russell Terrier.

However, defects do occur from time to time in certain lines, and, where this is the case, the breeder of the dog should always be notified. By informing the breeder, you will be giving them

Breeders strive to eliminate health problems from their lines.

the chance to take the appropriate action in their breeding plan.

It would be unfair to instantly blame the breeder of the dog if a problem has come to light. Defects are usually the result of a combination of recessive genes, and the puppy may have come from two apparently sound and healthy parents, put together in good faith. Such is the nature of dog breeding that unexpected defects will arise from time to time.

There are now tests available for many hereditary defects, and all Russells used for breeding should be subjected to testing for conditions that are know to occur in the breed. If a breeder continues to use a line that is known to produce defects, mating

PERTHE'S DISEASE

This is a disease that is not uncommon in small dogs, usually affecting the adolescent. A restriction in the blood supply to the femoral head results in damage to the bone. In mild cases, the condition will rectify itself. However, in more severe cases, surgical removal of the femoral head may be necessary. The affected dog will usually make a full recovery following surgery. The condition often comes to light following a knock to the hips, and may or may not be inherited.

affected dogs, the appropriate breed club should be notified. Most breed clubs have a code of ethics to which all members should adhere.

Primary Lens Luxation

A condition commonly seen in terriers. The supporting ligament of the lens may break as a result of trauma, but will more frequently be the result of an inherited defect. In most cases, the condition will lead to blindness.

Hereditary Cataract

Cataracts will cause the eye to become cloudy and commonly result in blindness.

The cataracts can, in certain cases, be operated on but with limited success.

Luxating Patella

Essentially a slipping kneecap, the condition will vary in severity, and affects the movement of the dog, which will be seen to 'skip' when walking.

IN SUMMARY

The Jack Russell Terrier is a breed second to none. Sporting, athletic, and full of character, you will have many years of happy companionship with your chosen pet. Remember to keep your half of the deal and provide the diet, health care and training that will enable your Russell to enjoy life to the full.

Once you have owned a Jack Russell, you will never want another breed.

ABOUT THE AUTHOR

John Valentine has owned Jack Russell Terriers since childhood, and has acquired a huge amount of knowledge on the breed. He has now bred seven generations of Jack Russells and has shown them with great success at Hunt Shows.

In 1990, the Parson Russell Terrier received official Kennel Club recognition in the UK, enabling enthusiasts to exhibit their dogs at Championship shows, including the prestigious Crufts show.

John has won many awards at Championship shows, and he also judges the breed at Championship level.